A Gu
MANHATTAN PROJECT
IN
MANHATTAN

Cynthia C. Kelly & Robert S. Norris

Introduction by Richard Rhodes

Introduction

The name "Manhattan Project" is commonly thought to be a red herring. In fact, the U.S. Army Corps of Engineers named the top-secret project as it did because its first offices were actually located in Manhattan, at 270 Broadway.

New York City served as a crucible for the physics, chemistry, metallurgy and engineering that led to the development of the world's first atomic bombs in World War II. On January 25, 1939, in the basement of Columbia University's Pupin Hall, Herbert Anderson used the university cyclotron to replicate the recently discovered phenomenon of nuclear fission—the first time fission was witnessed in the United States.

Nobel Prize-winning scientists Enrico Fermi, Harold Urey and I. I. Rabi, their colleagues Leo Szilard, John Dunning and others carried out pioneering research at Columbia in the code-named Substitute Alloys Materials (SAM) Laboratory. In the basement of Schermerhorn Hall, Enrico Fermi built a subcritical nuclear reactor of graphite and uranium. He called it a "pile" and used players from Columbia's football team to stack the heavy blocks of graphite. It served as a prototype for the full-scale pile Fermi later built in Chicago, which produced the world's first controlled nuclear chain reaction in December 1942.

By the end of 1943, chemist Harold Urey was directing more than 700 people investigating the technology of enriching uranium. At sites throughout Manhattan, some 5,000 New Yorkers contributed their knowledge and skills to the Manhattan Project.

This guide, complementing the exhibit *WWII & NYC* at the New-York Historical Society, unveils New York City's top-secret Manhattan Project sites. Enjoy a tour of this fascinating history.

Richard Rhodes, author, *The Making of the Atomic Bomb*

Table of Contents

Manhattan's Secret Sites

The Manhattan Project, the Anglo-American effort to build an atomic bomb during World War II, was one of the most significant—and secretive—undertakings of the 20th century. While most Manhattan Project operations were scattered across the country, New York City hosted a surprising number of projects.

Manhattan Project insignia

This guidebook takes readers to ten different Manhattan Project sites, from the science halls at Columbia University to the childhood home of J. Robert Oppenheimer, director of the Manhattan Project laboratory at Los Alamos, NM. General Leslie R. Groves, who oversaw the nationwide Manhattan Project, visited New York City about fifty times in the three years between his appointment as leader of the Manhattan Engineer District and the dropping of the bombs on Japan.

Traveling by train, Groves would meet with Corps of Engineers subordinates, corporate leaders who were designing or operating his atomic factories, or scientists and engineers who provided expert advice. A surprising number of New York City offices, laboratories, and warehouses were involved in the top-secret project. While these New York City sites remain largely unmarked and unknown, they were a small but crucial part of the success of the Manhattan Project, and deserve to remembered.

WHAT'S IN A NAME?

The name itself, "Manhattan Project," is commonly thought to be a misnomer. But the first offices of the Manhattan Project were actually in Manhattan, at 270 Broadway. General Leslie Groves decided to follow the custom of naming Corps of Engineers districts for the city in which they are located. Thus the atomic bomb project became known as the Manhattan Engineer District (MED) or "Manhattan Project." The title had the additional benefit of masking the actual purpose of the top-secret project.

SED
SPECIAL ENGINEER DETACHMENT

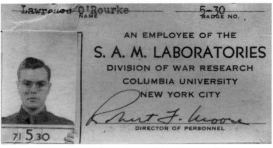

Lawrence O'Rourke's ID card for SAM Laboratory
Courtesy of Lawrence S. O'Rourke

In 1943, the Manhattan Engineer District could not find enough technically trained people to work at the various plants and laboratories involved in the atomic bomb project around the country.

On May 22, 1943, the Army created the Special Engineer Detachment to help fill the need. The SED came from 300 different universities and 47 states. Some SEDers, like Lawrence S. O'Rourke and William E. Tewes, first worked at the Substitute Alloy Materials (SAM) Laboratory at Columbia University or other sites in New York City developing the gaseous diffusion process before being transferred to Oak Ridge, TN. Colonel Kenneth D. Nichols praised the SED for its specialized talents and contributions. At a ceremony in December 2010 honoring SED members in Oak Ridge, veteran William J. Wilcox praised them as the "unsung heroes" of the Manhattan Project.

OUTNUMBERED BY CIVILIANS

"When I started [at Columbia], we [the SEDers] were very limited, maybe a dozen, but it grew to at least fifty. When the barrier started to be manufactured in at least three places, the development people in those sites would send in their samples, and we'd evaluate them at Columbia, as to their efficiency in separating the isotopes. And so we moved from the Pupin Physics Labs after about nine months and we moved up into an old automobile sales building up on Amsterdam Avenue [the Nash Garage Building]...We occupied four floors of that building and I imagine there were at least fifty of us at that time. We were outnumbered by civilians you see...There must have been at least 150 civilians in it."

~Lawrence S. O'Rourke, AHF oral history

Map

Title and address of former Manhattan Project site, with closest intersecting street. Closest subway station and line in italics.

1 **Nash Garage Building**
3280 Broadway at
W. 134 St.
137th St.-City College [1]

2 **Columbia University**
2960 Broadway
at W. 120th St.
116th St. - Columbia University [1]

3 **New York Buddhist Church**
331-332 Riverside Drive at W. 105th St.
103rd St. [1]

4 **Former Home of J. Robert Oppenheimer**
155 Riverside Drive at W. 88th St.
86th St. [1]

5 **Union Carbide and Carbon Corp. Building**
30 E. 42nd Street
at Madison Ave.
5th Avenue [7] or Grand Central [4, 5, 6, S]

6 **Madison Square Area Engineers Office**
261 Fifth Avenue
at 29th St.
28th Street [N, R, W]

7 **Baker and Williams Warehouses**
513-519, 521-527, and 529-535 W. 20th Street
at 10th Ave.
23rd Street [C, E]

8 **First Headquarters of the Manhattan Engineer District**
270 Broadway at
Chambers St.
City Hall [N, R, W] or Chambers Street [A, C]

9 **Kellex Corporation Headquarters**
233 Broadway at Park Place
Park Place [2,3]

10 **Office of Edgar Sengier**
25 Broadway at Morris St.
Bowling Green [4,5]

Atomic Basics
THE SCIENCE BEHIND THE BOMB

Everything around us is made of **atoms**. Atoms are the smallest units that make up **elements**. At the heart of the atom is the **nucleus**, which is made up of two kinds of subatomic particles: **protons**, with a positive electric charge, and **neutrons**, with no charge. **Electrons**, with a negative charge, orbit around the nucleus. The nucleus is bound together by an incredibly strong energetic force. When the nucleus splits, nuclear energy is released.

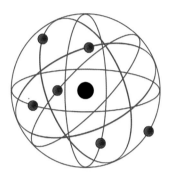

Photo courtesy of Colin M. Burtnett, Wikimedia Commons

Isotopes are different forms of the same element. They have the same number of protons and electrons but a different number of neutrons. Two naturally-occurring isotopes of uranium are **uranium-235** with 143 neutrons (235 heavy particles) and **uranium-238** with 146 neutrons (238 heavy particles).

Those extra three neutrons make all the difference. U-235 is much more unstable than U-238 and easily splits apart ("fissions") when hit by another neutron.

NUCLEAR TERMINOLOGY

Atom: building block of matter; made up of a small, dense nucleus surrounded by a cloud of negatively-charged **electrons.**

Nucleus: makes up the center of the atom; consists of a number of positively-charged **protons** and neutral **neutrons**. An atom is classified by the number of protons and neutrons in its nucleus.

Isotope: Isotopes of an element possess the same number of protons in their nuclei but have different numbers of neutrons.

Fission: the process by which an atom's nucleus is split into smaller pieces; results in the release of neutrons and lots of energy.

Pile: a nuclear reactor. Coined by Enrico Fermi at the Met Lab, it was based on the first rudimentary nuclear reactor which was nothing more than a pile of uranium and graphite blocks.

The atoms of most elements—like hydrogen, oxygen, iron, or lead— are stable. Their nuclei tend to stay together rather than break apart. But uranium-235 is different. When a nucleus of this isotope is hit by a speeding neutron, it **fissions**, or splits, into two smaller nuclei plus one to three extra neutrons—and releases a lot of energy. The extra neutrons smash into more nuclei, fissioning them and releasing even more neutrons in a cascade of incredible energy.

This is called a **nuclear chain reaction.** When controlled inside a re- actor, a chain reaction can use a small amount of U-235 or plutonium fuel to generate massive amounts of energy.

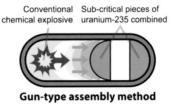

Gun-type assembly method

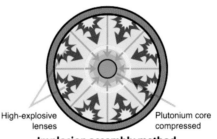

Implosion assembly method

Image courtesy of Wikimedia Commons

FAT MAN AND LITTLE BOY

In order to detonate a nuclear weapon, you need a **critical mass** of fissionable material to ensure that the neutrons released by fission will strike another nucleus and release its neutrons, producing a chain reaction. The more fissionable material you have, the greater the odds that such an event will occur.

The U.S. developed two types of atomic bombs during the Second World War using different fissionable materials--enriched uranium (U-235) and plutonium (Pu-239). Each bomb was designed to bring subcritical masses together to produce a critical mass. "**Little Boy**," dropped on Hiroshima, was a gun-type weapon with an enriched uranium core. "**Fat Man**," dropped on Nagasaki, was an implosion- type device with a plutonium core.

The Race for the Bomb

In a letter dated August 2, 1939, Albert Einstein warned President Franklin D. Roosevelt that Germany was probably working to produce an "extremely powerful" bomb. Einstein hoped to galvanize the United States into developing an atomic bomb before Hitler did.

Albert Einstein meets with Leo Szilard to compose his letter to FDR
Photo courtesy of the U.S. Department of Energy

In response to Einstein's letter and the urging of British prime minister Winston Churchill, President Roosevelt authorized a top-secret effort to build an atomic bomb. Organized as a military effort under the Army Corps of Engineers, scientists were recruited to work on the project from the leading universities and laboratories across the United States. In addition, scientists from Great Britain and Canada came as part of the British Mission led by Sir James Chadwick, who was awarded the Nobel Prize for his 1932 discovery of the neutron.

Dozens of refugees from Europe, many of them also Nobel Prize-winning scientists, joined the project. Together, physicists, chemists, engineers, mathematicians and other scientists designed, built and tested the world's first atomic bombs. Their drive to uncover nature's innermost secrets was combined with a sense of patriotic duty to contribute to the war effort.

Lise Meitner & Otto Hahn
Photo courtesy of the U.S. Department of Energy

LISE MEITNER: REFUGEE FROM THE NAZIS
Being Jewish, Lise Meitner was subject to the increasingly repressive anti-Semitic laws. Because so many Jewish intellectuals had already fled, in July 1938 German authorities forbade academics to emigrate. Leaving Berlin by train, Meitner barely escaped when Nazi officials inspected her expired Austrian passport at the Holland border. She continued her study of uranium atoms in exile in Sweden. Though slim and shy, Lise was a formidable physicist and found in her work an escape from her loneliness in exile.

11

Research related to an atomic bomb began long before World War II. As early as 1933, Hungarian Leo Szilard conceived of the possibility of a chain reaction, the explosive force that powers an atomic bomb. In 1934, Italian physicist Enrico Fermi and his team in Rome bombarded elements with neutrons. They split uranium, but did not realize it at the time.

At the Kaiser Wilhelm Institute in Berlin, Austrian physicist Lise Meitner and German chemists Otto Hahn and Fritz Strassmann studied Fermi's data. By accident, the German chemists discovered that uranium atoms bombarded by neutrons broke into lighter particles. Otto Hahn was so disturbed by the possible military implications of his discovery that he contemplated suicide.

In December 1938, Lise Meitner correctly read the Hahn-Strassmann experiments as evidence that the uranium nuclei had been split into new particles. Meitner, along with her nephew Otto Frisch, coined the term "fission" to describe what had occurred with the uranium nucleus. They drew an analogy to a water drop dividing in two. Meitner and Frisch also theorized the potential for a chain reaction and thus, an atomic bomb.

On January 26, 1939, Danish physicist Niels Bohr announced the discoveries of Lise Meitner and her German colleagues to a physics conference at the George Washington University in Washington, DC. After learning about "atomic fission," using uranium, some attendees immediately set up an experiment to replicate the results at the nearby Carnegie Institution of Washington and elsewhere. The race for the bomb had begun.

A RACE WITH HITLER'S SCIENTISTS

Glenn Seaborg was motivated by the urgency of World War II.

"Lots of signs made us think that we were in a losing race with Hitler's scientists. We understood full well what it would have meant if Adolf Hitler had got the atomic bomb before the Allies did."

Interview with Academy of Achievement
September 1990

The project's pace quickened with the selection of hard-driving U.S. Army Corps of Engineers General Leslie R. Groves to direct the project in September 1942. Groves had been in charge of all domestic Army construction needed to mobilize for the war, including the mammoth Pentagon building.

Groves was supremely self-confident, extraordinarily decisive and insightful. He was also an astute judge of people. Despite J. Robert Oppenheimer's past communist associations and lack of management experience, Groves recognized that Oppenheimer was critical to the success of the project and chose him as its scientific director.

Enrico Fermi, Leo Szilard and other top physicists joined the Manhattan Project effort at the Metallurgical Laboratory or "Met Lab" housed at the University of Chicago. Under the bleachers of Stagg Field, a university stadium, the world's first controlled, self-sustaining nuclear chain reaction took place in a squash court on December 2, 1942.

A drawing of the Chicago Pile-1
Image from AHF Archives

The Manhattan Project began as a small research program. At the outset, J. Robert Oppenheimer estimated that 100 scientists could do the research, design and testing at Los Alamos. But the endeavor proved to be far more complex, involving not just scientific research but a gargantuan engineering and industrial effort. Mammoth first-of-a-kind factories were built to produce the fissile material at the core of the bombs, enriched uranium and plutonium.

The hulking K-25 plant at Oak Ridge, TN, was a mile long, built to separate the isotopes of uranium using gaseous diffusion. A totally different approach involved huge "Calutrons," named after the University of California's newly invented "cyclotrons." These used electromagnetic forces to separate the isotopes. A third technique, thermal separation, required a third huge facility to produce enriched uranium. At Hanford, WA, three huge reactors and three chemical separation facilities were constructed to produce, separate and concentrate plutonium.

Dozens of small manufacturers, major corporations and universities contributed. Danish physicist Niels Bohr had observed that building an atomic bomb could never be done without turning the United States into one huge factory. Bohr saw his words borne out as the nationwide project transformed America with facilities coast-to-coast.

The B Reactor at Hanford
Photo courtesy of the U.S. Department of Energy

UPTOWN

Nash Garage Building
3280 BROADWAY

The Nash Garage Building started its life as something other than a purpose-built scientific facility. Had you been present at the building's ribbon cutting ceremony, you would not have found much high-tech scientific equipment. Instead, you would have seen long rows of gleaming Nash automobiles and nearly as many smiling salesmen. It was only later that Columbia University bought the auto dealership's space and converted its large interior into an industrial laboratory.

During the Manhattan Project, the building was turned into a pilot plant to create the barrier material for Oak Ridge's K-25 gaseous diffusion plant. K-25's diffuser cells separated the uranium isotope useful for weapons production (U-235) from its more common but less useful cousin (U-238) by forcing uranium-rich gas through a porous barrier material. The lighter U-235 molecules could pass through the barrier material more easily than the heavier U-238 molecules, eventually producing the desired concentration level of U-235.

The Nash Garage Building today

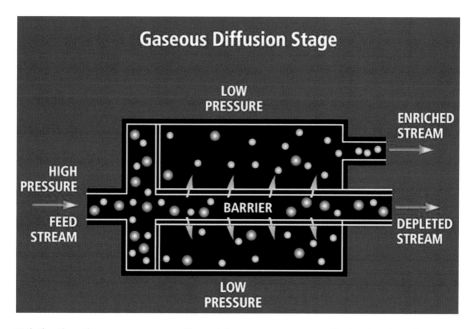

Gaseous Diffusion Stage

LOW PRESSURE

ENRICHED STREAM

HIGH PRESSURE

FEED STREAM

BARRIER

DEPLETED STREAM

LOW PRESSURE

While the theory surrounding this process was relatively simple, producing a functional barrier was another matter. The uranium-rich gas was highly corrosive, so the barrier material had to be tough as well as porous. Initially, research went forward on a method developed by two Columbia physicists, Edward Adler and Edward Norris, that used corrosion-resistant nickel. Later an improved method using powdered nickel was developed by a scientist named Clarence Johnson.

ASK ME NO QUESTIONS, I'LL TELL YOU NO LIES

"I graduated from high school at the age of fifteen and a half, and after one term of college and a year's experience in a chemical plant, I went to work for the Manhattan Project. In 1944, I was 17 years old when I became a Laboratory Assistant [in the Nash Garage Building] with no idea of what was the end product at this facility. As the lone African-American in the midst of these PhD scientists, I was not going to ask too many questions.

"My major job was to clean tubes in an acid solution. I did not know what these long tubes were made of. In retrospect, I believe the fabric that the tubes were made of was supposed to be tested as the means to separate the U-235 from the U-238. I was on vacation in 1945 when the first bomb was dropped and when I saw the headline I realized that I had been part of this extraordinary endeavor."

~James Forde, letter to AHF, June 27, 2012

Johnson worked for the Kellex Corporation. The teams focusing on the Adler-Norris and Kellex-Johnson methods worked feverishly to refine their techniques in time for the best process to be installed in the production facility being built in Decatur, Illinois. In the Nash Garage Building, the teams built a pilot plant as they attempted to determine whether their designs would function on an industrial scale. Eventually, General Groves decided to go with the Kellex-Johnson process. Half-installed Adler-Norris equipment was pulled from the Decatur plant and replaced with the newer method's apparatus.

The Nash Garage Building represents an early example of the alliance between the government, academia, and private industry that would come to characterize the Manhattan Project. Employees of the Kellex Corporation worked beside professors and graduate students from Columbia. They strove to accomplish the same goal and all worked at the behest of the U.S. government.

GUMMING UP THE WORKS

Dr. Edward Adler was invited to join the project at Columbia by Harold Urey. Only twenty-six in 1942, he was so enthusiastic about the project that he often literally lived in his Columbia laboratory. His partner, Edward Norris, was actually an English interior decorator, but he played a surprising and significant role in the quest to make gaseous-diffusion a reality. Frustrated by the inferiority of paint spray guns, Norris developed his own spray gun. His most innovative development was a very fine, metal mesh.

Working together, Adler and Norris devised a promising method to separate uranium isotopes. While their electroplated nickel design was rejected in favor of the powered nickel design of Johnson at Kellex, they laid the groundwork for the barrier that was used.

One of the more amusing moments of the Manhattan Project came when Adler commandered the printing press of the American Chicle Company, a gum manufacturer in Long Island City, to help with the barrier design. For months Adler used the press to print tiny ink dots, while enveloped by the smell of spearmint.

A 1905 ad for Chiclets gum
Photo courtesy of Wikimedia Commons

RELEGATED TO THE BASEMENT

Donald Trauger
Photo courtesy of the Oak Ridger

"I was at Columbia [working on the barrier material to separate the isotopes of uranium]...They took over an eight-story parking garage that was a few blocks downstream from Columbia University in Manhattan.

"Much of the project moved there. Since I was using fairly heavy equipment for providing the gas circulation and the exchange and all that was needed for testing the barrier, we wanted a good stable floor. So I was relegated to the basement, as I had been at Pupin Laboratory for similar reasons, I guess.

"That parking garage was converted to a very fine laboratory in a very short time, a few months."

~Donald B. Trauger, AHF oral history, September 22, 2005

The interior of K-25, where the gaseous diffusion process enriched uranium for the atomic bombs
Photo courtesy of the U.S. Department of Energy

Columbia University
2960 BROADWAY (PUPIN AND SCHERMERHORN HALLS)

Pupin Hall

Important Manhattan Project research was conducted at Columbia University's Pupin Hall and Schermerhorn Hall. World-class physicists, including Nobel Prize winners Isidor I. Rabi and Enrico Fermi, joined Columbia's research team to investigate the relatively new science of atomic particles. Hungarian physicist Leo Szilard first realized the possibility of a nuclear chain reaction in 1933, and against the backdrop of escalating hostilties in Europe, the race began to harness the enormous energy within the atom.

The basement laboratory of Pupin Hall became home to a cyclotron, a type of particle accelerator first invented in the early 1930s by Ernest O. Lawrence of the University of California. Known as "atom smashers," cyclotrons accelerate atoms through a vaccuum and use electromagnets to induce collisions at speeds up to 25,000 miles per second. The results of such experiments provided valuable clues about the behavior of atoms. The cyclotron in Pupin Hall's basement was built by Dr. John R. Dunning, an associate professor of physics, and Dr. George Pegram.

JOHN DUNNING: PUZZLE-SOLVER

Physicist John R. Dunning led the team that built Columbia's first cyclotron. During the Manhattan Project, Dunning led day-to-day operations and research at the Substitute Alloy Materials Lab (SAM), the codename for Columbia's secret nuclear laboratory. There he developed the gaseous diffusion method of uranium isotope separation, still used today, and established himself as an authority in nuclear engineering. Many believed the program was too technically daunting to be completed. The program's success is a testimony to Dunning's intellect and love for solving complicated problems.

In January 1939, Columbia's cyclotron made history. Physicists in the United States had just received word that German scientists Otto Hahn and Fritz Strassmann had bombarded uranium atoms with neutrons and observed that the uranium seemed to split into atoms of smaller elements. They shared their results with Austrian physicists Otto Frisch and Lise Meitner, who termed the phenomenon "nuclear fission."

Columbia physicists rushed to replicate the experiment using the cyclotron in Pupin Hall. A team of scientists including Dunning, Herbert Anderson, Eugene Booth, and Francis Slack were the first Americans to split the uranium atom and demonstrate the enormous release of

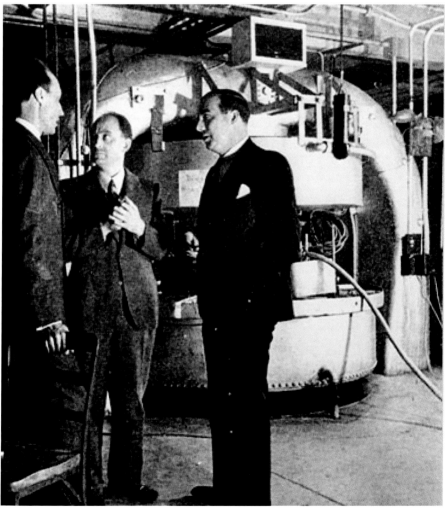

Physicists John Dunning, Enrico Fermi, & Dana P. Mitchell by the Columbia cyclotron
Photo courtesy of AIP Emilio Segrè Visual Archives

energy that resulted. Fermi helped to plan the experiment, but was in Washington, DC, for a physics conference. On the night of January 25, 1939 Dunning recorded the monumental event in his diary: "Believe we have observed new phenomenon of far-reaching consequences." The work at Columbia confirmed "nuclear fission" and provided further evidence for the possibility of creating a nuclear chain reaction.

The following year, Columbia scientists first proved that the fissionable material in uranium that released energy when bombarded with neutrons was the isotope uranium-235. However, uranium-235 is a rare isotope, comprising about 0.7 percent of naturally-occurring uranium ore. Uranium-235 isotopes needed to be separated from the more prevalent uranium-238 isotopes and concentrated to about 90 percent for use in a nuclear weapon.

A scientific team at Columbia, including Dunning and chemist Harold Urey, invented and perfected the "gaseous diffusion" method of separating uranium isotopes. During the Manhattan Project, a gaseous diffusion plant known as K-25 was built and operated at Oak Ridge, Tennessee. Until recent years, gaseous diffusion was the primary method used to obtain uranium-235. The Columbia cyclotron was used for experiments until 1965. Portions of the machine are now at the Smithsonian Institution in Washington, DC, and will be on display as part of the New-York Historical Society's exhibition, *WWII & NYC*.

GASEOUS DIFFUSION PROCESS: DOOMED TO FAIL?

Harold Urey, who won the Nobel Prize for Chemistry, was Director of War Research at Columbia University from 1940 to 1945. At the secret nuclear laboratory, Urey worked with Dunning, Percival Keith, and Manson Benedict to design a gaseous diffusion process that would be built in the enormous K-25 plant at Oak Ridge.

Photo courtesy of Wikimedia Commons

Urey and his team were struggling to find a "barrier material" and feared the gaseous diffusion process was doomed to fail. While General Groves was critical of Urey's administrative skills, a material was found and the process worked. A great scientific mind, Urey went on to do pioneering work on "cosmochemistry" and the origins of planets.

RUNNING INTO SCIENTISTS ALL OVER THE PLACE

Darragh Nagle first became involved in the Manhattan Project as a graduate student at Columbia. He went on to work at the Metallurgical Laboratory at the University of Chicago and at Los Alamos.

"[Herbert Anderson and I] were pretty good friends [at Columbia]. Herb was Enrico Fermi's principal assistant at that time. He and Fermi did experiments in the buildings around the campus, Pupin Laboratory especially but also Schermerhorn was another...

"There were all these distinguished people: Fermi, Urey, the Mayers, Nordsick, Rabi, Anderson...And then when I moved to Chicago there they all were again, and then when I moved to Los Alamos there they all were again plus some other new eminences: Oppenheimer, and we saw Niels Bohr and other people around. But I saw them from afar, we weren't privy to their work."

~*Darragh Nagle , AHF oral history, August 2003*

Schermerhorn Hall

New York Buddhist Church
331-332 RIVERSIDE DRIVE

The historic statue of Shinran Shonin, founder of the Jodo Shinshu school of Buddhism, stands in front of the New York Buddhist Church. This statue of Shinran Shonin survived the atomic bombing of Hiroshima, Japan on August 6, 1945. Nearly 150,000 people were killed by the explosion and its aftermath, and 90 percent of the buildings in the city collapsed or burned.

Known as "Little Boy," the bomb used on Hiroshima contained uranium produced in Oak Ridge, Tennessee. Scientists working at Los Alamos, New Mexico, perfected the the design of the device, a "gun-type" assembly that fired one piece of uranium-235 into another to generate a powerful explosion. The bomb was assembled on Tinian Island in the Pacific and loaded on to the B-29 bomber *Enola Gay*, piloted by Colonel Paul W. Tibbets and crewed by members of the 509th Composite Group.

At approximately 8:15 AM, "Little Boy" was dropped on the port city and major military headquarters, exploding at about 1,900 feet over the city. A mushroom cloud rose miles above Hiroshima, and the estimated temperature at the center of the blast was over a million degres centigrade. Observing the blast, *Enola Gay* co-pilot Robert Lewis wrote: "My God, what have we done?"

***Enola Gay*, the plane that dropped the atomic bomb on Hiroshima**
Photo courtesy of the U.S. Department of Energy

On August 9, 1945, a second atomic bomb, containing plutonium produced at Hanford, Washington, was dropped on Nagasaki, Japan. Several days later, Emperor Hirohito offered his unconditional surrender to Allied forces. Much has been written about the decision to use the atomic bomb on Japan, and the issue remains controversial today. For more information about the decision to use the bomb, the Cold War arms race, and nuclear weapons today, please see the list of suggested readings in the back of this book.

The statue of Shinran Shonin at the New York Buddhist Church (below) is now the focus of an annual peace gathering held on August 5. A bell is tolled at 7:15 PM (Eastern Time), corresponding to the moment in Japan when the Hiroshima bomb was dropped.

JOHN HERSEY'S *HIROSHIMA*

John Hersey's *Hiroshima* was first published in the August 31, 1946 issue of *The New Yorker*. The issue was entirely devoted to the article and sold out within hours. While earlier accounts of the bombing focused on the more abstract, physical effects of the blast, Hersey's article is compellingly personal, relating the experiences of six people in haunting and painful detail. In Hersey's account, one survivor surveys the immediate aftermath of the bombing:

"From the mound, Mr. Tanimoto saw an astonishing panorama. Not just a patch of Koi, as he had expected, but as much of Hiroshima as he could see through the clouded air was giving off a thick, dreadful miasma. Clumps of smoke, near and far, had begun to push up through the general dust. He wondered how such extensive damage could have been dealt out of a silent sky; even a few planes, far up, would have been audible. Houses nearby were burning."

Hiroshima in the aftermath of the atomic bomb
Photo courtesy of the U.S. Department of Energy

The atomic bomb over Nagaski
Photo courtesy of the U.S. Department of Energy

Oppenheimer's Childhood Home
155 RIVERSIDE DRIVE

An apartment spanning the entire 11th floor of 155 Riverside Drive was the childhood home of theoretical physicist J. Robert Oppenheimer. During the Manhattan Project, Oppenheimer was director of the Los Alamos Laboratory and responsible for the research and design of an atomic bomb.

The Oppenheimers moved into the building shortly after Robert was born on April 22, 1904. His father, Julius Oppenheimer, had emigrated from Germany in 1888 and became a successful businessman in the fabrics industry. His mother, Ella, was an accomplished painter and art professor at Barnard College. Robert's childhood apartment was lavishly decorated with fine European furniture and art, including works by Pablo Picasso, Pierre-Auguste Renoir, Paul Cézanne, and Vincent Van Gogh.

Oppenheimer's family was part of the Ethical Culture Society, an outgrowth of American Reform Judaism founded and led at the time by Dr. Felix Adler. The progessive society placed an emphasis on social justice, civic responsibility, and secular humanism.

The Ethical Culture School today

Dr. Adler also founded the Ethical Culture School at 33 Central Park West (now the Fieldston School), where Oppenheimer enrolled in September 1911. His academic prowess was apparent very early on, and by the age of 10, Oppenheimer was studying minerals, physics, and chemistry. His correspondence with the New York Mineralogical Club was so advanced that the Society invited him to deliver a lecture—not realizing that Robert was a twelve-year-old boy!

He graduated as valedictorian of his high school class in 1921, but fell ill with a near-fatal case of dysentery and was forced to postpone enrolling at Harvard until September 1922. After being bedridden for months, his parents arranged for him to spend the summer of 1922 in New Mexico, a haven for health-seekers.

Robert stayed at a dude ranch 25 miles northeast of Santa Fe with high school teacher Herbert Smith as a companion and mentor. From there, he took five- or six-day horseback trips in the wilderness. This experience restored Oppenheimer's health and instilled a deep love for the desert high country. He returned to northern New Mexico repeatedly, bringing his brother Frank and many friends.

The majestic Pajarito Plateau in NM that so enraptured young Robert Oppenheimer

Because of his health issues, Oppenheimer had been forced to postpone enrolling at Harvard until September 1922. He graduated in three years, excelling in a wide variety of subjects. Although he majored in chemistry, Oppenheimer eventually realized his true passion was the study of physics.

Photo courtesy of AHF Archives

In 1925, Oppenheimer began his graduate work in physics at Cavendish Laboratory in Cambridge, England. J. J. Thomson, who had been awarded the 1906 Nobel Prize in Physics for detecting the electron, agreed to take on Oppenheimer as a student. At Cavendish, Oppenheimer realized that his talent was for theoretical, not experimental, physics, and he accepted an invitation from Max Born, director of the Institute of Theoretical Physics at the University of Göttingen, to study with him in Germany.

Oppenheimer had the good fortune to be in Europe during a pivotal time in the world of physics, as European physicists were then developing the groundbreaking theory of quantum mechanics. Oppenheimer received his doctorate in 1927 and accepted professorships

Oppenheimer and Ernest O. Lawrence
Photo courtesy of AIP Emilio Segrè Visual Archives

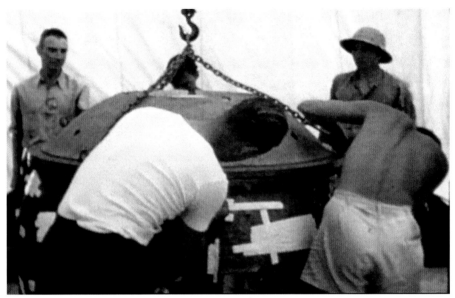

Oppenheimer and Los Alamos scientists preparing "Gadget" before the Trinity test
Photo courtesy of the U.S. Department of Energy

at the University of California, Berkeley, and the California Institute of Technology. At Berkeley, he became good friends with Ernest O. Lawrence, one of the world's top experimental physicists and the inventor of the cyclotron. Lawrence named his second son after Robert.

By the time the Manhattan Project was launched in the fall of 1942, Oppenheimer was already considered an exceptional theoretical physicist and had become deeply involved in exploring the possibility of an atomic bomb. Throughout the previous year he had been doing research on fast neutrons, calculating how much material might be needed for a bomb and how efficient it might be.

Although Oppenheimer had little managerial experience and some troublesome past associations with Communist causes, General Leslie Groves recognized his exceptional scientific brilliance. Less than three years after Groves selected Oppenheimer to direct weapons development, the United States dropped two atomic bombs on Japan, leading to Japan's unconditional surrender. As director of the Los Alamos Laboratory, Oppenheimer proved to be an extraordinary choice.

After the war and until his death in 1967, Oppenheimer directed the Institute for Advanced Study in Princeton, New Jersey, where he convened great scientists. "What we don't understand, we explain to each other."

J. Robert Oppenheimer and General Leslie R. Groves at the Trinity test site
Photo courtesy of the U.S. Department of Energy

MIDTOWN

Union Carbide & Carbon Corp. Building
30 EAST 42ND STREET

Though now marked by a new office building, the southwest corner of Madison Avenue and 42nd Street was once home to the headquarters of an important Manhattan Project contractor: the Union Carbide and Carbon Corporation. From this building, the company's leaders directed a diverse group of activities that were crucial to the success of the bomb project.

The Murray Hill Area Engineers Office and the Union Mines Development Corporation were on the 18th floor of the building. Much of Union Carbide's involvement in the Manhattan Project dealt with the processing and enrichment of uranium, but before that could be done, raw uranium ore was needed. The Union Mines Development Corporation was formed as a subsidiary of Union Carbide to purchase uranium ore from domestic sources. If they had any questions about what was needed, they could simply walk down the hall to the Murray Hill Engineers Office, the Army agency charged with coordinating all uranium procurement for the project.

Union Carbide played an important role in ore procurement, but their largest contribution to the Manhattan Project was operating the gigantic K-25 gaseous diffusion plant in Oak Ridge, Tennessee. The gaseous diffusion process separated the more useful uranium-235 isotope from less useful uranium-238 by forcing both through a barrier material (see "Nash Garage Building" on page 16 to learn more).

THE LARGEST BUILDING IN THE WORLD
At the time K-25 was finished, it was the largest roofed building in the world. The mile-long, U-shaped plant covered forty-four acres and employed 12,000 workers. Union Carbide was tasked with ensuring that everything operated as efficiently and secretly as possible.

**Oak Ridge housing was designed in several prefabricated models,
designated by letters of the alphabet and assigned based on rank and family size.**
Photo by Ed Wescott. Courtesy of the U.S. Department of Energy

The gaseous diffusion process was effective, but it took thousands of repetitive "cascades" to produce even the smallest increase in the concentration of U-235 or enriched uranium. Thus, a gigantic facility was required to house the 3,000 stages of diffusion equipment and 12,000 people working in around-the-clock shifts.

Secrecy and security were a top priority at Oak Ridge. Every man, woman and child living or working in the city was required to have an ID badge. By 1945 over 5,000 security guards, military police, and civilian policemen were patrolling Oak Ridge and its borders to ensure that no secrets were leaked.

Labor was in short supply during the war, so Union Carbide had to undertake a rather unconventional policy: it hired women! Before the war, women commonly worked as secretaries, nurses, or schoolteachers. Now the K-25 plant employed numerous women, many of them just out of high school or college, to help test and operate the gaseous diffusion equipment.

**An operator in the Y-12 plant
in Oak Ridge**
Photo courtesy of Ed Westcott

Madison Square Engineers Office
261 FIFTH AVENUE

Inside this unassuming office building, a team of approximately 300 people worked to procure materials needed for the atomic bomb, such as uranium, graphite, and beryllium. The office was run by Lieutenant Colonel John R. Ruhoff until September 1944, when Major Wilbur E. Kelly took over.

The work carried out in the Madison Square Area Engineers Office was an example of how General Groves divided up the seemingly infinite tasks into manageable, discrete pieces. This approach was critcal to the success of the enormously ambitous project.

On December 2, 1942, Enrico Fermi's team produced the first controlled nuclear chain reaction, Chicago Pile-1. Built in a squash court at the University of Chicago, the reactor was a lattice of 400 tons of graphite, 58 tons of uranium oxide, and six tons of uranium metal.

Scientists realized that if a nuclear chain reaction could be packaged as a bomb, it could produce an explosion thousands of times more violent than any conventional explosives. Whoever built the first atomic bomb could bring an end to World War II and possibly all future world-scale wars, as J. Robert Oppenheimer predicted.

The task of the Madison Square Area Engineers Office was to obtain industrial quantities of the materials for top-secret nuclear reactors, enrichment plants and other facilities essential to the development of the atomic bomb at Hanford, WA, Oak Ridge, TN, Los Alamos, NM, and other sites across the country.

In order to achieve this, Groves pushed hard for the highest priority for procuring materials for the project. On his second day on the job, Groves walked into the War Production Board and demanded that the Manhattan Project's rating be upgraded from AA3 to AAA, the highest designation.

Donald Nelson, then head of the War Production Board, refused. Starting to leave Nelson's office, Groves said he would have to recommend to the President that the project be abandonded because the War Production Board was unwilling to cooperate. Nelson gave in and signed Groves' letter assigning the Manhattan Project AAA priority status.

This AAA status gave Manhattan Project scientists and personnel an extraordinary advantage. Colonel Paul W. Tibbets, Jr., the head of the 509th Composite Group or the weapons delivery arm of the Manhattan Project, used the AAA status to great effect. Using the codeword "Silverplate," Tibbets was able to commandeer specially modified B-29s, the best air crews, and the use of Wendover Airfield in Utah for training. Throughout the project, the AAA priority rating was integral to its success.

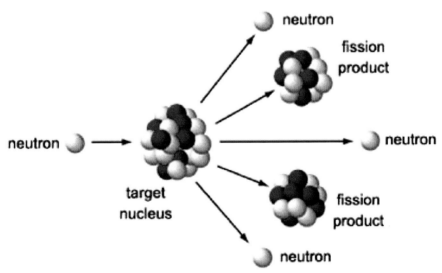

In this diagram, the nucleus of an atom is bombarded by a neutron and undergoes fission, splitting apart into fission products and neutrons. In a chain reaction, the neutrons generated by this initial fission reaction trigger additional fission reactions. If enough neutrons and target nuclei are present, the chain reaction can sustain itself, producing a tremendous amount of energy.
Image courtesy of the U.S. Department of Energy

Baker & Williams Warehouses
513-19, 521-27, 529-35 WEST 20TH STREET

The cavernous Baker and Williams warehouses (left) were used by the Manhattan Engineer District in the early 1940s for the short-term storage of tons of uranium concentrates that had been shipped in secret to the nearby Hudson River docks. The ore was then distributed to government facilities involved in nuclear reactor and atomic weapons programs.

The processed uranium came from the Eldorado Mining and Refining Limited company in Canada, which had large stocks of uranium as waste from its radium refining activities. To accommodate American and British orders and maintain secrecy, Eldorado was purchased by the Canadian government. By 1946 more than 4,000 tons of ore concentrate containing approximately 1,100 tons of uranium oxide had been delivered to the MED.

Although the acquisition of sufficient quantities of uranium was vital to the success of the Manhattan Project, there was no guaranteed plan for how to best separate it. Separation of uranium isotopes on an industrial scale was a critical step in the bomb manufacture.

General Leslie Groves, head of the Manhattan Engineer District, was technically shrewd, had complete confidence in his own judgment, and was willing to take enormous risks with untried processes. Under pressure to produce a bomb before the end of the war, Groves decided to pursue alternative approaches in parallel until one or another was proven successful. At Oak Ridge, TN huge plants were contructed using three different methods: gaseous diffusion, thermal separation, and electromagnetic separation. Centrifugal separation techniques were not yet fully developed.

Each method had its advocates, but none was proven. As it happened, none of the processes alone produced enough enriched uranium, but when used in tandem, they were successful.

First, the partially or 1% to 2% enriched product from the thermal process was used as feedstock for the gaseous diffusion process. This process succeeded in producing 20% enrichment. Next the product was fed into the electromagnetic separation plants, which achieved the 90% enrichment needed for a bomb. Thus, the uranium that had once been stored in the Baker and Williams Warehouses as low-grade ore was processed for use in the "Little Boy" bomb.

Uranium was not the only material used for making atomic bombs. Plutonium was discovered by Glenn Seaborg's research group in February 1941. They realized that plutonium could be produced from uranium by bombarding it with neutrons. This process was launched on an industrial scale in huge nuclear reactors in Hanford, WA. The Hanford facilities eventually produced the plutonium for the "Fat Man" bomb dropped on Nagasaki, Japan.

**Uranium that has been extracted from ore, refined, and pressed
into a circular unit called a "billet"**
Photo courtesy of the U.S. Department of Energy

The Times Square Building
229 WEST 43RD STREET

Although the flow of information about the Manhattan Project was tightly controlled, *New York Times* reporter William L. Laurence was allowed unique access to the inner workings of the project.

A Lithuanian immigrant who fled Russia in 1905, Laurence graduated from Harvard Law School before becoming a reporter. In an article published in September 1940, "The Atom Gives Up," he foresaw the awesome potential of harnessing atomic energy.

Photo courtesy of Real Estate Weekly

Laurence's article was so alarmingly prescient that in 1943, General Leslie Groves ordered that anyone borrowing the article from a library be reported to him. Edward Adler (see page 17) ended up on the "suspect" list after checking out the article to learn more about gaseous diffusion.

In April 1945, Groves decided to retain the services of a reporter and asked the managing editor of the *New York Times* to provide Laurence. At the time, the newspaper was headquarted in the Times Square Building. The arrangement worked out well for both sides: the *Times* got the scoop of the century, and the Manhattan Project got an enthusiastic advocate for atomic energy.

Laurence witnessed key historic moments, including the Trinity test near Alamagordo, NM, on July 16, 1945. He was upset that he was forced to remain twenty miles away from Ground Zero but drafted his own obituary—just in case. Among his notes, he described Edward Teller applying sunscreen to prepare for the blast.

Laurence was also on Tinian Island in the Pacific for the depature and return of the *Enola Gay* from its mission over Hiroshima on August 6, 1945. He commissioned Robert Lewis, co-pilot of the *Enola Gay*, to write a log of the flight. At the last minute, Laurence was allowed on *The Great Artiste*, the instrument plane that accompanied *Bockscar* on its mission to drop "Fat Man" over Nagasaki on August 9, 1945.

Laurence's position as both insider and reporter gave him a unique perspective of the Manhattan Project. His good relationship with General Groves, scientists, and members of the 509th Composite Group and his brilliant writing style cemented him as the chronicler of the project.

Nicknamed by his *New York Times* colleagues "Atomic Bill," Laurence continued to write about the potential of atomic energy until his death in 1977.

 The New York Times.

"All the News That's Fit to Print"

LATE CITY EDITION
Partly cloudy, less humid today. Cloudy and warm tomorrow.
Temperatures Yesterday—Max., 72; Min., 66
Sunrise today, 5:37 A. M.; Sunset, 8:00 P. M.

Copyright, 1945, by The New York Times Company.

VOL. XCIV..No. 31,972.   Entered as Second-Class Matter, Postoffice, New York, N. Y.   NEW YORK, TUESDAY, AUGUST 7, 1945.   THREE CENTS NEW YORK CITY

FIRST ATOMIC BOMB DROPPED ON JAPAN; MISSILE IS EQUAL TO 20,000 TONS OF TNT; TRUMAN WARNS FOE OF A 'RAIN OF RUIN'

Unlocking the "Cosmic Cupboard" of Atomic Power

On May 16, 1945, Laurence submitted a draft radio address to be delivered by President Truman after the first atomic bomb was dropped over Japan. However, Groves did not approve the speech, and all copies—save one—were destroyed. Eventually the job of drafting Truman's speech was given to Arthur W. Page, Vice President of Marketing for AT&T and a close friend of Secretary of War Henry Stimson.

Patricia Cox Owen, who worked in General Groves' inner office, saved the only surviving copy of Laurence's fifteen-page draft address. The excerpts below underscore Laurence's hope that atomic energy would bring immense improvements in "the health, wealth and happiness of all mankind, ushering in a new era of prosperity."

"Today marks one of the most important days in the history of our country and of the world. Today...our 20th Air Force has released upon Japan the most destructive weapon ever developed by any nation.

William L. Laurence and General Groves
Photo courtesy of the Patricia Cox Owen Collection

"This greatest of all weapons, developed exclusively by American genius, ingenuity, courage, initiative and farsightedness on a scale never ever remotely matched before, will, no doubt, shorten the war by months, or possibly even years. It will thus save many precious Amerian lives and much treasure. But, while the work was undertaken primarily for the purpose of developing a weapon for the winning of the war against Japan in the quickest possible time and at the smallest possible cost in lives, the tremendous concentrated power contained in the new weapon also has enormous possibilities as the greatest source of cosmic power ever to be tapped by man, utilizing the unbelievable quantities of energy locked up within the atoms of the material universe...

"Under proper control, this new force now placed at our disposal—the equivalent of tens of millions of trained men—can become the greatest weapon for enforcing peace that the world has ever known, insuring a period of peace lasting into the far distant future, and conceivably until such a time when every individual or nation on earth will have attained such a high moral sense that war will have become unthinkable.

"We are now so far ahead that it would take any other nation from ten to twenty-five years to catch up with us. We must, and we will, see to it, that we maintain our lead. As long as we do not relax our efforts and make sure that no nation ever gets ahead of us, or even matches us, we can be certain that our defenses are in good order and that no would-be aggressor would dare act against our will to maintain peace...

"We have produced enough of these bombs to lay waste to every one of their [Japan's] cities and to cause such havoc in the rest of their country that it will be a wilderness for generations to come. We therefore put this choice squarely before them: 'Either surrender unconditionally or be destroyed'. If they persist in their madness and continue to take a toll in American lives in a senseless continuation of a war that they themselves have known for a long time they must inevitably lose, the burden of responsibility for their own destruction will rest squarely on their own shoulders...

The New York Times.

LATE CITY EDITION

VOL. XCIV. No. 31,974. NEW YORK, THURSDAY, AUGUST 9, 1945. THREE CENTS

SOVIET DECLARES WAR ON JAPAN; ATTACKS MANCHURIA, TOKYO SAYS; ATOM BOMB LOOSED ON NAGASAKI

"Atomic energy, if controlled by the major peace-loving nations, should insure the peace of the world for decades to come and possibly for many generations. If misused, it can lead to the wiping out of our civilization...

"Providence has placed its trust in the American people by providing us with the key that unlocks this 'Cosmic Cupboard' of Atomic Power, and the American people will keep faith with this trust. We will do with this new continent what we did with this land of ours—develop it and cultivate it until we reach a new Promised Land of wealth, health, and happiness for all mankind, ushering in a new era of prosperity such as the world has never seen. With God's help and guidance we will achieve this goal."

43

New York Times reporter William L. Laurence and Jesse Kupferberg on Tinian Island
Photo courtesy of the Walter Goodman Collection

DOWNTOWN

First Headquarters of the MED
270 BROADWAY

At first glance, "Manhattan Project" appears to be a strange code name for an undertaking that took place across the country. After all, the bomb design was done in Los Alamos, NM; the uranium enrichment process in Oak Ridge, TN; and the plutonium production in Hanford, WA. Why name the entire endeavor after New York City's most famous borough?

The answer lies at 270 Broadway (right), in what is now the Arthur Levitt State Office Building. In 1942, the 18th floor of the building was the headquarters of the North Atlantic Division of the Army Corps of Engineers. This building became the project's first headquarters in mid-June of 1942. In August 1943, the headquarters were shifted to the rapidly growing Manhattan Project site in Oak Ridge, TN.

The name initially proposed for the project was the "Laboratory for the Development of Substitute Materials." Worried that it revealed too much about the project's intentions, General Groves preferred the "Manhattan Engineer District" (MED), named after the location of its initial offices.

Unlike other Corps of Engineers units, the new District did not administer a geographic area but rather coordinated a multisite project spanning the entire country. Appointed to direct the project in September 1942, Groves preferred to operate from Washington, DC and had offices in the New War Building, completed in June 1941.

While 270 Broadway's most notable contribution to the Manhattan Project was serving as its first headquarters, Stone & Webster, a Boston-based engineering firm, also had offices in the building. Stone & Webster was tasked with building the Y-12 electromagnetic separation plant to produce enriched uranium. This method was one of the three different approaches pursued at the Oak Ridge, TN site.

The electromagnetic separation method was the most developed of the potential ways to produce fissile material at the start of the Manhattan Project. Ernest O. Lawrence, working at the University of California-Berkeley, determined that when an electrically-charged atom was placed in a magnetic field, it would trace a circular path with a radius determined by the atom's mass. U-235 was lighter than U-238 and could be isolated by placing a collecting pocket in its path.

The massive Y-12 plant at Oak Ridge was designed to carry out on a large scale what Lawrence had successfully done in his Berkeley lab.

At the Y-12 plant in Oak Ridge, equipment known as an "Alpha" racetrack was used to electromagnetically separate isotopes of uranium
Photo courtesy of the U.S. Department of Energy

While the machines in California were called cyclotrons, at Y-12 they were dubbed "calutrons" from *CALifornia University cyclo-TRONs*. Ground was broken for the Tennessee facility on February 18, 1943.

At Y-12, there were 1,152 separate calutron units or tanks that resembled the capital letter "D." The Alpha calutrons consisted of 96 very large tanks arranged in a giant ellipse called a "racetrack."

Oak Ridge worker Otis Sharpe counts silver pieces retrieved from Y-12
Photo courtesy of the U.S. Department of Energy

The Beta calutrons had 36 tanks that were half the size of Alpha tanks and were arranged in a rectangle. Because of wartime shortage of copper, the huge magnetic coils had to be wound with 14,700 tons of silver obtained from the U.S. Treasury.

Tennessee Eastman Corporation recruited mostly girls just out of high school as operators. Not told what they were producing, they

AN ABUNDANCE OF SILVER

Copper was in short supply during the war, so Y-12's electromagnetic coils were made largely using silver. Where could one find nearly the 15,000 tons of silver necessary for the project? The government's vaults, of course.

When a Manhattan Project official asked Assistant Secretary of the Treasury Daniel Bell for 6,000 tons of the metal, Bell retorted, "Young man, *you* may think of silver in tons, but the Treasury will always think of silver in troy ounces." Enough troy ounces were located and Y-12 was a success.

After the war, all of the silver fragments were carefully retrieved from the machinery and returned to the Department of Treasury. In the end, only 0.036% of the borrowed silver was missing.

worked in cubicles and carefully adjusted control knobs to maximize output. They were called "cubicle girls" (back then the term "calutron" was secret). Known now as the "calutron girls," the women proved in a week-long test to have a better feel for how to adjust the knobs to optimize production than PhD physicists. The physicists, constantly fiddling with the controls, lost the competition.

Despite initial troubles, the Y-12 plant eventually produced enriched uranium for the first atomic bomb. But the calutrons required an exorbitant amount of energy and over 22,000 employees. In December 1946, all of the Y-12 calutrons were shut down except for the Beta 3 calutrons and the pilot units in Building 9731.

Starting in 1959, the Beta 3 calutrons were used to produce over 200 stable isotopes used for cancer treatment, medical diagnostics, non-proliferation, and other applications. In 1998, production was shut down but today the control room and other portions of the facility remain as they were in 1945.

Manhattan Project workers outside the Y-12 Plant in Oak Ridge, TN
Photo courtesy of Ed Westcott

Kellex Corporation Headquarters
233 BROADWAY (WOOLWORTH BUILDING)

The Woolworth Building
Photo courtesy of Aude, Wikimedia Commons

The 60-story Woolworth Building was the tallest habitable structure in the world from 1913 until the Empire State Building eclipsed it in 1931. During the Manhattan Project, the Kellex Corporation had its offices in the Woolworth Building. Kellex was created as a separate entity of the M. W. Kellogg Company to preserve the secret nature of the company's wartime work in Manhattan.

PERCIVAL KEITH: AN OPTIMIST FOR GASEOUS DIFFUSION

Percival (Dobie) Keith was vice president of engineering at Kellogg and the founder of Kellex ("Kell" for Kellogg and "X" for secret). Keith was self-confident, energetic, and driven. He was optimistic about the success of the gaseous diffusion process and assured General Groves that it was possible. Keith, who enjoyed challenges, assembled an all-star team of scientists and relentlessly pushed the project to success. His personality and professional skills proved instrumental in achieving a functioning gaseous diffusion process.

The M.W. Kellogg Company, headquarted in Jersey City, NJ, specialized in chemical engineering projects and had worked with General Groves prior to the war on an ordnance plant in Louisiana. This experience prompted Groves to offer the company a contract to design and supervise construction of the massive K-25 gaseous diffusion plant in Oak Ridge, TN. The plant was designed to separate isotopes of uranium and produce enriched uranium. Kellex accepted the contract in December 1942.

Construction of the K-25 plant, designed by Kellex
Image from AHF Archives

THE KIND OF MAN WE WANT

Dr. Clarence Johnson was in charge of experimental research at Kellex. The son of Swedish immigrants, Johnson was a hard worker from a young age. Dobie Keith, upon learning of Johnson's academic record and work ethic, exclaimed, "Hire Clarence Johnson immediately! That's the kind of man we want." At Kellex, in charge of a huge laboratory staffed by 200 men, Johnson developed the first square foot of uranium isoptope barrier material; miraculously, the new material passed all the tests on June 19, 1944. Without this barrier material, gaseous diffusion would not have been possible.

Kellex chose the Woolworth Building as it was convenient to the headquarters of the Manhattan Engineer District. In addition, Kellex built a pilot gaseous diffusion plant for Columbia University in the Nash Garage Building. Architects had to design the K-25 plant at the same time as scientists and engineers were refining the technology that would go into the building.

The massive K-25 Plant in Oak Ridge, TN
Photo courtesy of the U.S. Department of Energy

TRANSLATING "K-25"

When General Groves contracted M. W. Kellogg Company to design the top-secret plant, Kellogg created the Kellex Corporation. The plant site was named "K-25" with "K" for Kellex and "25" for "U-235." "25" was a common designation for U-235 during the project.

Sir James Chadwick
Photo courtesy of Wikimedia Commons

In 1944, at the height of the project, the Kellex Corporation had nearly 3,700 employees. The K-25 plant in Oak Ridge cost $512 million to build, or $6.5 billion today. The mile-long, U-shaped plant covered forty-four acres, was four stories high and up to 400 feet wide. Engineers developed special coatings for the hundreds of miles of pipes and equipment to withstand the corrosive uranium hexaflouride gas that would pass through the plant's 3,000 repetitive diffusion stages.

The Woolworth Building temporarily housed many European refugees who were part of the British Mission. Led by Sir James Chadwick, the British Mission consisted of a couple dozen scientists who eventually worked at the laboratory in Los Alamos, NM. Their talent and expertise were essential to the success of the Manhattan Project.

A SPY FOR THE SOVIETS

Physicist Klaus Fuchs arrived in New York in December 1943 as part of the British Mission. For nine months, he worked at the Kellex headquarters on the gaseous diffusion process. His espionage began in New York, where he provided the Soviets with information about gaseous diffusion technology, including the composition of the vital "barrier material."

Klaus Fuchs
Photo courtesy of Wikimedia Commons

In August 1944, Fuchs went to Los Alamos, where he was involved in highly important theoretical work. Fuchs provided the Soviets with classified information, including a description of the plutonium bomb, the mechanism used to detonate the bomb, and the mass of plutonium required.

Fuchs confessed to spying in 1950 and served nine years in prison. The information from Fuchs and two other spies allowed the Soviets to obtain an atomic bomb approximately one to two years earlier than they would have without the aid of espionage.

Office of Edgar Sengier
25 BROADWAY (CUNARD BUILDING)

This Renaissance Revival building got its name in 1921 when it became the New York headquarters for Cunard Steamship Line, the renowned British trans-atlantic shipping and travel company. The building was also the base of operations for Edgar Sengier, who passed through the ornately decorated, maritime-themed lobby each day to reach his office.

Sengier was director of the Société Générale, one of the largest companies in Belgium, and the Union Minière du Haut Katanga, a mining company in the Belgian Congo. Soon after the discovery of the fission of uranium atoms in early 1939, Sengier realized that uranium ore could be a crucial ingredient in making an atomic bomb. Uranium ore from his Shinkolobwe mine was very rich, containing up to 65% uranium. In contrast, Canadian ore contained only 0.02%.

If the uranium ore fell into the wrong hands, the consequences could be disastrous. Alarmed by the Nazi occupation of Belgium, Sengier shipped tremendous quantities of uranium ore across the Atlantic. Nearly 1,250 metric tons of uranium ore in over 2,000 drums—half the uranium stock available in Africa—were shipped and secretly stored in the Archer Daniels Midland Warehouses in Staten Island.

After the start of the war, Sengier moved Union Minière's worldwide operations to New York. In the spring of 1942, Sengier notified the government that he had a cache of valuable uranium ore stored in

New York City. His letters to Thomas K. Finletter, special assistant to the Secretary of State in the Division of Defense Metals, received no response for several months.

Immediately after General Leslie Groves took over the project on September 17, 1942, he ordered Colonel Kenneth D. Nichols to meet with Sengier. Just ten days earlier, Nichols had learned from Finletter that there was a stockpile of uranium already in the United States of unknown quantity and quality.

On September 18, Nichols purchased the entire Staten Island supply, as well as another 3,000 tons from Union Minière's mine in Africa. The large quanitites of high-grade uranium was a fortuitous windfall for the Manhattan Project.

In 1946, General Groves presented Sengier the Medal for Merit for his contribution to the war effort. He was the first non-American civilian to receive this distinction. The citation simply reads for "services in supplying material," as there were still many restrictions on what information could be released.

General Leslie Groves with Edgar Sengier and Brigadier General John Jannarone
Photo courtesy of Robert S. Norris

A PROJECT BUILT ON FEAR

One of General Groves' closest aides in Washington, DC, Major Robert F. Furman was an engineering graduate from Princeton who had worked with Groves on building the Pentagon and on other projects. In mid-July 1945, Furman personally escorted the uranium projectile for the "Little Boy" bomb from Los Alamos to Tinian Island.

Furman was also part of the Alsos Mission. Begun in September 1943, the mission was to discover how far the Italians, French, and Germans had gotten in their atomic bomb projects, interrogate scientists, and impound equipment and supplies. The following is an excerpt from Furman's account of his experience.

"The name [Alsos] was a mystery name for the whole war. And for ten years after the war nobody could figure out where the name came from. Eventually I had to tell them that the colonel that I worked with was a Greek student, and "alsos" is a Greek word for groves, grove of trees. If General Groves had known that, I would have been put up to the firing squad because he didn't want any secret like that to get known. But it's sort of an interesting little quirk of how this colonel got the project properly named after all...

"The Manhattan Project was built on fear: fear that the enemy had the bomb, or would have it before we could develop it...

Robert Furman receiving the Legion of Merit from General Groves in December 1945
Photo courtesy of the Patricia Cox Owen Collection

Allied soldiers with the German experimental reactor pile at Haigerloch in April 1945
Photo courtesy of Wikipedia

"This scientific mission [Alsos] was very effective. As the army moved forward it interviewed German scientists—all kinds of scientists, French, Belgian, whatever—and picked up information as to what the Germans were doing. One of the most important reports they wrote was called the Strasbourg Report, which really told General Groves and President Roosevelt that they [the Germans] didn't have a project. They were focusing on rockets...

"Don't forget, if [the Japanese] had a project, we knew it would have to be a tremendous project like Oak Ridge. If somebody showed us a 40,000 foot warehouse and said that was their project, why, we felt pretty safe because Oak Ridge was a million feet. Our project was half the size of the state of Rhode Island. As far as we knew, nobody could do it any quicker or any faster, although that was one of our fears, that maybe somebody would figure out a way to produce an atomic bomb in a different way than we were doing it.

"Particularly in Korea, where they had mineral resources, we checked out all the mines to see if there was an interest in mining uranium, or thorium, radium. That's where it would all have to start. From this, we could make our report back that [Japan had] no serious project."

~*Robert Furman, AHF oral history, February 20, 2008*

V-E Day in NYC

Dear Mom,

Like several million more people, I believe this has been the best couple of days in several years. There has been quite a bit of unusual talk over the radio, connected with V.E. Day celebrations. I've heard some rather bitter remarks from particularly gloomy people (civilian or otherwise) who rave and fume at any sort of joyous exposition. Then, on the other hand, there does exist the few who have gone a little too far in considering the war completely over...

Dick Reed and I spent several hours among the half million people in Times Square last night...Many, many policemen kept the crowds moving more or less; however, very few cars attempted to chance the mob. Hundreds of photographers were snapping picutres from all possible angles. One little kid climbed high upon a war bond sign to get in a picture; he could not make it down so a mounted policeman had to effect the rescue. A very striking sight occurred when a whole platoon of Free French sailors marched right down the middle of everything, singing the "Marseilles".

After spending 45 minutes in navigating the single, short block in front ot the Astor, Dick and I took the ferry over to Staten Island. The torch of "The Lady" was blazing for the first time since the start of the war. That was really a memorable and beautiful sight. Even with the dim-out (to be lifted tonight) New York's skyline was breathtaking!

Tonight, over the radio, I heard the sound as they rang the Liberty Bell from Independence Hall in Philadelphia.

Love, Buddy [Ralph Gates]

Shortly thereafter, Ralph Gates, Harvey Willard, and Dick Reed were shipped off to the Manhattan Project at Oak Ridge and Los Alamos.

A World War II poster extolling Americans to fight on
Photo courtesy of the National Archives

Chronology
THE MAKING OF THE ATOMIC BOMB

1899	New Zealand physicist Ernest Rutherford identifies two kinds of natural radiation: alpha particles and beta rays.
1905	Albert Einstein proposes a theory, shown most dramatically in a nuclear explosion, that defines the relationship between energy and mass: $E=mc^2$.
1932	British physicist James Chadwick discovers the neutron.
1933	Hungarian physicist Leo Szilard first conceives of a nuclear chain reaction and the potential for an atomic bomb.
1934	Italian physicist Enrico Fermi and his team in Rome bombard elements with neutrons and split uranium but do not realize it.
1938	Otto Hahn and Fritz Strassmann, German physicists, discover the fission process by splitting uranium in two. Austrian physicists Lise Meitner and Otto Frisch coin the term "nuclear fission" and publish results.
1939	Danish physicist Niels Bohr announces recent discoveries about fission by European colleagues at an international conference on theoretical physics in Washington, DC.
Aug. 2, 1939	Einstein sends a letter to President Franklin D. Roosevelt warning of the prospect of Germany developing an atomic bomb.
Sept. 1, 1939	Nazi Germany invades Poland; World War II begins.
June 1940	The National Defense Research Committee (NDRC) is established to organize U.S. scientific resources for war, including research on the atom and the fission of uranium.
Feb. 24, 1941	American scientist Glenn T. Seaborg's research team discovers plutonium.
June 22, 1941	Nazi Germany invades the Soviet Union.

Oct. 9, 1941	President Roosevelt asks the Chairman of the NDRC, Vannevar Bush, to determine the cost of an atomic bomb and explore construction needs with the Army.
Dec. 7, 1941	Japan attacks Pearl Harbor.
Dec. 8, 1941	The United States Congress declares war on Japan.
Dec. 10, 1941	Germany and Italy declare war on the United States.
Jan. 19, 1942	President Roosevelt approves the production of an atomic bomb.
Aug.13, 1942	General order is issued by the Chief of Engineers formally establishing the Manhattan Engineer District (MED) for construction of an atomic bomb.
Sept. 17, 1942	Colonel Leslie R. Groves takes over command of the MED.
Sept. 19, 1942	Groves selects Oak Ridge, TN, as the site for a pilot plant for uranium isotope separation.
Nov. 25, 1942	Groves selects Los Alamos, NM, as the scientific research laboratory, codenamed "Project Y." J. Robert Oppenheimer is chosen as laboratory director.
Dec. 2, 1942	Fermi's team produces the first sustained nuclear fission chain reaction under the bleachers at University of Chicago's Stagg Field.
Jan. 16, 1943	Groves selects Hanford, WA, as a site for plutonium production.
July 17, 1944	Major reorganization to maximize plutonium implosion research occurs at Los Alamos after the plutonium gun-type bomb is abandoned.
April 12, 1945	Franklin D. Roosevelt dies and Harry S. Truman becomes President.
April 25, 1945	Groves and Secretary of War Henry Stimson brief Truman on the Manhattan Project.
May 7, 1945	Nazi Germany surrenders to the Allies.

June 6, 1945	Stimson and other members of the Interim Committee recommend to President Truman that the atomic bomb be used as soon as possible without warning.
June 1945	The Franck Report, urging demonstration of the bomb before military use, begins circulating among scientists.
July 16, 1945	Trinity test, the first nuclear explosion, is successfully conducted in Alamogordo, NM.
July 17, 1945	Potsdam Conference of President Truman, Prime Minister Winston Churchill and Communist Party General Secretary Joseph Stalin begins.
July 21, 1945	Truman approves order for the use of atomic bombs.
July 24, 1945	Truman informs Stalin that the United States has developed a powerful new weapon.
July 26, 1945	Potsdam Declaration asks Japan for unconditional surrender and warns of "prompt and utter destruction."
July 29, 1945	Japan rejects the Potsdam Declaration.
Aug. 6, 1945	The Little Boy uranium bomb is dropped on Hiroshima, Japan.
Aug. 9, 1945	The Fat Man plutonium bomb is dropped on Nagasaki, Japan.
Aug. 14, 1945	Japan surrenders.
Jan. 24, 1946	The United Nations adopts its first resolution, which establishes the United Nations Atomic Energy Commission.
May 21, 1946	Louis Slotin receives a lethal dose of radiation conducting an experiment at Los Alamos. He dies on May 30, 1946.
Aug. 1, 1946	President Truman establishes the Atomic Energy Commission (AEC), which assumes responsibility for all property in the custody and control of the MED.
Aug. 15, 1947	The Manhattan Engineer District is abolished.

Sources
AND FURTHER READING

Albright, Joseph and Marcia Kunstel. *Bombshell: The Secret Story of America's Unknown Atomic Spy Conspiracy*. New York: Times Books, 1997.

Bernstein, Jeremy. *Oppenheimer: Portrait of an Enigma*. Chicago: Ivan R. Dee, 2004.

Bird, Kai and Martin Sherwin. *American Prometheus: The Triumph and Tragedy of J. Robert Oppenheimer*. New York: Alfred A. Knopf, 2005.

Broad, William J. "Why They Called It the Manhattan Project." *The New York Times*, October 30, 2007.

Brown, Andrew. *The Neutron and the Bomb: A Biography of Sir James Chadwick*. Oxford: Oxford University Press, 1997.

Conant, Jennet. *109 East Palace: Robert Oppenheimer and the Secret City of Los Alamos*. New York: Simon & Schuster, 2005.

Fermi, Laura. *Atoms in the Family: My Life with Enrico Fermi*. Chicago: University of Chicago Press, 1954.

Frank, Richard B. *Downfall: The End of the Imperial Japanese Empire*. New York: Penguin Books, 1999.

Gosling, F. G. *The Manhattan Project: Making the Atomic Bomb*. United States Department of Energy, Energy History Series, 1994.

Groeuff, Stephane. *Manhattan Project: The Untold Story of the Making of the Atomic Bomb*. Boston: Little, Brown and Company,1967.

Groves, Leslie R. *Now It Can Be Told: The Story of the Manhattan Project*. New York: Harper, 1962.

Hasegawa, Tsuyoshi. *Racing the Enemy: Stalin, Truman, and the Surrender of Japan*. Cambridge: The Belknap Press, 2005.

Herken, Gregg. *Brotherhood of the Bomb*. New York: Henry Holt and Company, 2002.

Hersey, John. *Hiroshima*. New York: Alfred A. Knopf, 1985.

Kanon, Joseph. *Los Alamos*. New York: Dell, 1997.

Kelly, Cynthia C., ed. *The Manhattan Project: The Birth of the Atomic Bomb in the Words of Its Creators, Eyewitnesses and Historians*. New York: Black Dog & Leventhal, 2007.

Kelly, Cynthia C., ed. *Oppenheimer and the Manhattan Project: Insights into J. Robert Oppenheimer, "Father of the Atomic Bomb."* New Jersey: World Scientific, 2006.

Kelly, Cynthia C., ed. *Remembering the Manhattan Project: Perspectives on the Making of the Atomic Bomb and its Legacy*. New Jersey: World Scientific, 2004.

Lanouette, William. *Genius in the Shadows: A Biography of Leo Szilard, The Man Behind the Bomb*. Chicago: University of Chicago Press, 1992.

Norris, Robert S. *Racing for the Bomb: General Leslie Groves, the Manhattan Project's Indispensable Man*. South Royalton, Vermont: Steerforth Press, 2002.

Rhodes, Richard. *The Making of the Atomic Bomb*. New York: Simon & Schuster, 1986.

Walker, J. Samuel. *Prompt and Utter Destruction: Truman and the Use of Atomic Bombs Against Japan*. Chapel Hill: University of North Carolina Press, 1997.

Walker, Samuel. *Shockwave: Countdown to Hiroshima*. New York: Harper Collins, 2005.